A Paines Plough, Th[...]
Orange Tree Theat[...]

OUT OF LOVE

by Elinor Cook

The first performance of *Out Of Love* took place on
12 July 2017 in Paines Plough's Roundabout at Theatr Clwyd

PAINES PLOUGH

ARTS COUNCIL
Supported using public funding by
ARTS COUNCIL
ENGLAND

Theatr
Clwyd

Orange
Tree
Theatre

Out Of Love

by Elinor Cook

Cast

GEORGE/CHARLIE/LEONARD/DAD/ MIKE/TED/CHRISTOPHER/SAM	Hasan Dixon
LORNA/PENNY	Sally Messham
GRACE/RUTH	Katie Elin-Salt

Production Team

Direction	James Grieve
Lighting	Peter Small
Sound	Dominic Kennedy
Movement	Jennifer Jackson
Programmer	Joe Izzard
Assistant Director	Emily Ling Williams
Line Producer	Francesca Moody
Dramaturg	Guy Jones
Company Stage Manager	Linnea Fridén Grønning
Technical Stage Manager	Callum Thomson
2nd Technical Stage Manager	Hamish Ellis

ELINOR COOK (Writer)

Elinor Cook was the winner of the George Devine Award for Most Promising Playwright in 2013. She is currently writing a new version of Ibsen's *The Lady from the Sea* for the Donmar Warehouse, directed by Kwame Kwei-Armah. She is under commission to the Gate Theatre and Warwick Arts Centre.

Her plays include *Extra Yarn* (Orange Tree); *Pilgrims* (HighTide/Theatr Clwyd/The Yard); *The Rehearsal* (LAMDA); *Ten Weeks* (Paines Plough/Royal Welsh College of Music and Drama); *Image of an Unknown Young Woman* (Gate); *The Boy Preference* (NT Connections); *The Girl's Guide to Saving The World* (HighTide); *this is where we got to when you came in* (Bush/non zero one). She wrote an episode of *The Secrets* for BBC One, directed by Dominic Savage.

She was a member of Paines Plough's The Big Room and the Royal Court Supergroup in 2012. Prior to her writing career, Elinor worked as the senior reader at the Royal Court Theatre 2007–2009.

HASAN DIXON (George, Charlie, Leonard, Dad, Mike, Ted, Christopher & Sam)

Hasan trained at Central School of Speech and Drama.

Theatre includes: *War Horse* (National Theatre); *Carry On Jaywick* (HighTide); *Eventide*, *The Spanish Tragedy* (Arcola); *Re:Home* (The Yard); *Fear of Music* (Up in Arms/Out of Joint); *The Alchemist* (Liverpool Playhouse); *The Glass Menagerie* (Everyman); *Yerma* (Gate/Hull Truck); *You: The Player* (West Yorkshire Playhouse); *Ghosts* (UK tour); *The Return* (Southwark Playhouse).

Film & TV includes: *A Touch of Frost* (ITV); *Doctors*, *Silent Witness*, *Call the Midwife* (BBC); *This Is Not Happening* (Picnic Films) *And John Carter* (Disney/Pixar).

SALLY MESSHAM (Lorna & Penny)

Sally trained at RADA.

Theatre includes: *Tipping the Velvet* (Lyric Hammersmith); *The Sugar Wife*, *Women of Twilight*, *After Miss Julie* (RADA).

Film & TV includes: *Allied* (Gk Films); *Denial* (Krasnoff/Forster Entertainment); *Midwinter of the Spirit* (ITV Studios for ITV); *The Miniaturist* (The Forge Entertainment).

KATIE ELIN-SALT (Grace & Ruth)

Katie Elin-Salt trained at Royal Welsh College of Music and Drama.

Theatre includes: *Twelfth Night* (Shakespeare's Globe); *A Comedy of Errors* (National Theatre tour); *Crouch Touch Pause Engage* (Out of Joint/National Theatre of Wales); *Symphony* (nabokov/Soho); *Under Milk Wood*, *Season's Greetings*, *Educating Rita*, *As You Like It* (Theatr Clwyd); *Snow White and the Seven Dwarves* (Regent Theatre); *Cinderella* (Leeds City Varieties); *The Rise and Fall of Little Voice* (Bolton Octagon); *Holly and Ivan's Christmas Adventure* (Lyric Hammersmith); *Stealing Sweets and Punching People* (Nu-Write); *Love Steals Us From Loneliness* (National Theatre of Wales).

Television includes: *Stella* (Tidy Productions/Sky 1); *Doctors* (BBC TV); *Flash Prank* (Splash Media/MTV); *Tissues and Issues* (BBC); *And Perfect Summer* (Fiction Factory).

JAMES GRIEVE (Direction)

James is Joint Artistic Director of Paines Plough. He was formerly co-founder and Artistic Director of nabokov, and Associate Director of the Bush Theatre.

For Paines Plough James has directed *The Angry Brigade* by James Graham, *Broken Biscuits* and *Jumpers for Goalposts* by Tom Wells, *Hopelessly Devoted* and *Wasted* by Kate Tempest, *An Intervention* and *Love, Love, Love* by Mike Bartlett, *Fly Me To The Moon* by Marie Jones, *Tiny Volcanoes* by Laurence Wilson, *You Cannot Go Forward From Where You Are Right Now* by David Watson, *The Sound of Heavy Rain* by Penelope Skinner, *Organised* by Lucinda Burnett and *Happiness* by Nick Payne for BBC Radio 3. Further credits include a new production of *Les Misérables* for Wermland Opera in Karlstad, Sweden; *Translations* (Sheffield Theatres/ETT/Rose – winner Best Production, UK Theatre Awards 2014); *66 Books: A Nobody* by Laura Dockrill, *The Whisky Taster* by James Graham, *St Petersburg* by Declan Feenan and *Psychogeography* by Lucy Kirkwood (Bush); *Artefacts* by Mike Bartlett (nabokov/Bush, national tour & Off-Broadway); *Kitchen*, *Bedtime for Bastards* and *Nikolina* by Van Badham (nabokov).

PETER SMALL (Lighting)

Peter studied Lighting Design at The Royal Academy of Dramatic Art.

Musical theatre includes: *Cinderella* (Loughborough Theatre); *Tom & Jerry* (EventBox Theatre, Egypt); *All or Nothing* (UK national tours/Crescent/Vaults); *The Venus Factor* (Bridewell).

Theatre includes: *Bard on Board* (Cunard Queen Mary 2); *A Midsummer Night's Dream* (Forum Alpbach, Austria); *In the Gut* (Brighton Festival/Blue Elephant Theatre/Clown Fest 2016); *Electric* (Rio Cinema); *Our Teacher is a Troll* (UK tour/Paines Plough); *She Called Me Mother* (UK tours); *Crazy Lady, Free Association* (Forum Alpbach); *East End Boys and West End Girls* (Arcola/UK tour); *Politrix* (Hackney Showroom); *Almost Near* (Finborough); *Richard III* (Cunard Queen Mary 2); *The Witch of Edmonton* (Vanbrugh Theatre); *The Daughter-in-Law* (George Bernard Shaw Theatre); *Mother Theresa is Dead* (Gielgud).

Dance includes: *STEPLive! 2016* (Sadler's Wells); *STEPLive! 2017* (Royal Festival Hall); A Night with Gravity Circus (Jacksons Lane).

Concerts include: *A Night With Jason Robert Brown* (Royal Festival Hall).

Events include: *The Art of the Steal* (Louisa Guinness Gallery); *Never Such Innocence* (Australia House).

Associate/Assistant/Relight work includes: *Tiger Bay* (Cape Town Opera/Wales Millennium Centre); *Everybody's Talking About Jamie* (Sheffield Crucible); *Love, Lies and Taxidermy* (Theatre Clwyd); *Kiss Me Kate* (Théâtre du Châtelet/Grand Theatre Luxembourg); *Pink Confetti* (Babel International Festival); *Gianni Schicchi* (Teatro Real Opera House); *East is East* (Trafalgar Studios 1); *Thérèse Raquin* (Park/Finborough); *Arabian Nights* (Cunard Queen Mary 2); *The Realness* (Hackney Show Rooms).

DOMINIC KENNEDY (Sound)
Dominic Kennedy is a Sound Designer and Music Producer for performance and live events, he has a keen interest in developing new work and implementing sound and music at an early stage in a creative process. Dominic is a graduate from Royal Central School of Speech and Drama where he developed specialist skills in collaborative and devised theatre making, music composition and installation practices. His work often fuses found sound, field recordings, music composition and synthesis. Dominic has recently designed for and collaborated with Paines Plough, Engineer, Goat and Monkey, Jamie Wood, Gameshow, Manchester Royal Exchange, Outbox, Jemima James and Mars Tarrab. Recent installation work includes interactive sound design for *Gingerline* (pop-up restaurant pioneers) and the launch of Terry Pratchett's *The Shepherd's Crown*. Recent design credits include: *Broken Biscuits* (Paines Plough/Live Theatre Newcastle/nationwide

tour); *Growth* (Paines Plough/nationwide tour); *Love, Lies and Taxidermy* (Paines Plough/Theatr Clwyd/Sherman Theatre/nationwide tour); *I Got Superpowers For My Birthday* (Paines Plough/Half Moon/nationwide tour); *With a Little Bit of Luck* (Paines Plough/Latitude Festival/nationwide tour); *The Human Ear* (Paines Plough/nationwide tour); *The Devil Speaks True* (nationwide tour); *Run* (New Diorama); *Ono* (Soho); *Crocodiles* (Manchester Royal Exchange).

JENNIFER JACKSON (Movement)
Jennifer trained at East 15 and is a movement director and actor. Movement direction includes: *The Mountaintop* (Young Vic); *Death of a Salesman* (Royal & Derngate); *The Ugly One* (Park); *Phone Home* (Shoreditch Town Hall); *Why the Whales Came* (Southbank Centre); *Wuthering Heights* (workshop – Manchester Royal Exchange); *Stone Face* (Finborough); *Debris* (Southwark Playhouse/OpenWorks); *Macbeth* (Sam Wanamaker Playhouse/Passion in Practice); *Silent Planet* (Finborough); *Pericles* (Berwaldhallen, Stockholm); *Subterranean Sepoys* (New Diorama); *The Future* (The Yard); *Other* (*Please Specify*); *Atoms* (Company Three); *Takeover 2017* (Tricycle). Jennifer was the assistant movement director to Kate Sagovsky on the Paines Plough Roundabout season 2014 (Fringe First Winners), and is an associate artist with OpenWorks Theatre, Upstart Theatre, and a member of Tangled Feet.

As a performer Jennifer has worked with the NT, NT Studio, BAC, Bath Theatre Royal, Royal & Derngate Theatre, Sam Wanamaker Playhouse, Theatre 503, Arcola, Openworks Theatre, Derby Theatre, The Yard, The Harold Pinter Theatre (West End), Southwark Playhouse, Bervaldhallen (Stockholm), Lucas Theatre (Savannah, USA), Pearl Theatre (New York).

EMILY LING WILLIAMS (Assistant Director)
Emily was the assistant director on *The Island Nation* (Arcola, 2016). She completed Introduction to Directing and Springboard at The Young Vic during which she directed *Lungs* (Platform/Young Vic, 2016).

Emily has read scripts for Heyday Films, Origin Pictures and Blueprint Pictures.

She trained on the Acting Foundation Course at RADA before graduating from UCL with a BA in Philosophy.

Alongside directing she is also doing an MSc in Comparative Political Thought at SOAS and is on the Soho Theatre Writers Lab.

PAINES PLOUGH

Paines Plough is the UK's national theatre of new plays. We commission and produce the best playwrights and tour their plays far and wide. Whether you're in Liverpool or Lyme Regis, Scarborough or Southampton, a Paines Plough show is coming to a theatre near you soon.

'The lifeblood of the UK's theatre ecosystem' *Guardian*

Paines Plough was formed in 1974 over a pint of Paines bitter in the Plough pub. Since then we've produced more than 170 new productions by world renowned playwrights like Stephen Jeffreys, Abi Morgan, Sarah Kane, Mark Ravenhill, Dennis Kelly and Mike Bartlett. We've toured those plays to hundreds of places from Manchester to Moscow to Maidenhead.

'That noble company Paines Plough, de facto national theatre of new writing' *Daily Telegraph*

Over the last two years we've produced 22 shows and performed them in 180 places across four continents. We tour to more than 30,000 people a year from Cornwall to the Orkney Islands; in village halls and Off-Broadway, at music festivals and student unions, online and on radio, and in our own pop-up theatre Roundabout.

With Programme 2017 we continue to tour the length and breadth of the UK from clubs and pubs to lakeside escapes and housing estates. Roundabout hosts a jam-packed Edinburgh Festival Fringe programme and brings mini-festivals to each stop on its nationwide tour, and you can even catch us on screen with *Every Brilliant Thing* available on Sky Atlantic and HBO.

'I think some theatre just saved my life' @kate_clement on Twitter

PAINES PLOUGH · ROUNDABOUT

'A beautifully designed masterpiece in engineering… a significant breakthrough in theatre technology.' The Stage

Roundabout is Paines Plough's beautiful portable in-the-round theatre. It's a completely self-contained 168-seat auditorium that flat packs into a single lorry and pops up anywhere from theatres to school halls, sports centres, warehouses, car parks and fields.

We built Roundabout to enable us to tour to places that don't have theatres. For the next decade Roundabout will travel the length and breadth of the UK bringing the nation's best playwrights and a thrilling theatrical experience to audiences everywhere.

Over the last three years Roundabout has toured to 17 places, hosted 1,600 hours of entertainment for more than 65,000 people.

Roundabout was designed by Lucy Osborne and Emma Chapman at Studio Three Sixty in collaboration with Charcoalblue and Howard Eaton.

WINNER of Theatre Building of the Year at The Stage Awards 2014

'Roundabout venue wins most beautiful interior venue by far @edfringe.'
@ChaoticKirsty on Twitter

'Roundabout is a beautiful, magical space. Hidden tech make it Turkish-bath-tranquil but with circus-tent-cheek. Aces.'
@evenicol on Twitter

Roundabout was made possible thanks to the belief and generous support of the following Trusts and individuals and all who named a seat in Roundabout. We thank them all.

TRUSTS AND FOUNDATIONS
Andrew Lloyd Webber Foundation
Paul Hamlyn Foundation
Garfield Weston Foundation
J Paul Getty Jnr Charitable Trust
John Ellerman Foundation

CORPORATE
Universal Consolidated Group
Howard Eaton Lighting Ltd
Charcoalblue
Avolites Ltd
Factory Settings
Total Solutions

Pop your name on a seat and help us pop-up around the UK:
www.justgiving.com/fundraising/roundaboutauditorium

www.painesplough.com/roundabout
#roundaboutpp

Paines Plough

Joint Artistic Directors	James Grieve
	George Perrin
Senior Producer	Hanna Streeter
General Manager	Aysha Powell
Producer	Francesca Moody
Assistant Producer	Sofia Stephanou
Administrator	Simone Ibbett-Brown
Marketing and Audience	
Development Officer	Jack Heaton
Production Assistant	Harriet Bolwell
Finance and Admin Assistant	Charlotte Walton
Technical Director	Colin Everitt
Trainee Director	Emily Ling Williams
Production Placement	Alexandra Sikkink
Marketing Placement	Anushka Chakravarti
Admin Placement	Yuhan Zhang
Channel 4 Playwright in Residence	Zia Ahmed
Press Representative	The Corner Shop
Graphic Designer	Michael Windsor-Ungureanu
	Thread Design

Board of Directors

Caro Newling (Chair), Kim Grant, Nia Janis, Dennis Kelly, Matthew Littleford, Anne McMeehan, Christopher Millard, Cindy Polemis and Andrea Stark.

Paines Plough Limited is a company limited by guarantee and a registered charity.
Registered Company no: 1165130
Registered Charity no: 267523

Paines Plough, 4th Floor, 43 Aldwych, London WC2B 4DN
+ 44 (0) 20 7240 4533
office@painesplough.com
www.painesplough.com

 Follow @PainesPlough on Twitter

 Like Paines Plough at facebook.com/PainesPloughHQ

 Follow @painesplough on Instagram

Donate to Paines Plough at justgiving.com/PainesPlough

Theatr Clwyd

'One of the hidden treasures of North Wales, a huge vibrant culture complex' *Guardian*

Theatr Clwyd is one of the foremost producing theatres in Wales – a beacon of excellence looking across the Clwydian Hills yet only forty minutes from Liverpool.

Since 1976 we have been a theatrical powerhouse and much-loved home for our community. Now, led by Tamara Harvey and Liam Evans-Ford, we are going from strength to strength producing world-class theatre, from new plays to classic revivals.

We have three theatres, a cinema, café, bar and art galleries and, alongside our own shows, offer a rich and varied programme of visual arts, film, theatre, music, dance and comedy. We also work extensively with our local community, schools and colleges and create award-winning work for, with and by young people. In our fortieth year we will have co-produced with the Wales Millennium Centre, Sherman Theatre, Gagglebabble and The Other Room in Cardiff, Paines Plough, Vicky Graham Productions at the Yard Theatre, High Tide, Hampstead Theatre, Bristol Old Vic, The Rose Theatre, Kingston, Headlong and Sheffield Theatres.

Over 200,000 people a year come through our doors and in 2015 Theatr Clwyd was voted the Most Welcoming Theatre in Wales.

ARTISTIC DIRECTOR
Tamara Harvey
EXECUTIVE DIRECTOR
Liam Evans-Ford
ASSOCIATE PRODUCER
William James
ASSISTANT PRODUCER
Nick Stevenson
THEATRE ADMINISTRATOR
Melanie Jones
EXECUTIVE ASSISTANT
Tracy Waters
CAPITAL DEVELOPMENT
ASSOCIATE Pat Nelder

CREATIVE ENGAGEMENT
DIRECTOR OF CREATIVE
ENGAGEMENT
Gwennan Mair Jones
CREATIVE ENGAGEMENT
ASSOCIATE Emyr John
CREATIVE ENGAGEMENT
CO-ORDINATOR
Nerys Edwards
TUTORS Laura Heap,
Liz Morris, Clare-Louise
Rhys-Jones
SUPPORT WORKERS Chris
Ablett, Phoebe Dacre, Dave
Humphreys, Gaenor Williams

FINANCE
DIRECTOR OF FINANCE
Emma Sullivan
FINANCE CO-ORDINATOR
Sandra Almeida
FINANCE ASSISTANT
Carol Parsonage

GALLERIES
GALLERY CURATOR
Jonathan Le Vay

**MARKETING AND
COMMUNICATIONS**
DIRECTOR OF MARKETING
AND COMMUNICATIONS
Sam Freeman
SALES MANAGER
Marie Thorpe
PRESS AND
COMMUNICATIONS
COORDINATOR
Anthony Timothy

DIGITAL AND
COMMUNICATIONS
COORDINATOR
Angharad Madog
DESIGN AND DIGITAL
ASSISTANT Crayg Ward
SALES MERCHANDISER
Carole Jones
SALES ASSISTANTS Deborah
Charles, Catrin Davies, Carol
Edwards, Elaine Godwin,
Gwennan Henstock,
Rosemary Hughes,
Rhiannon Isaac, Nikki Jones,
Angela Peters, Jean Proctor,
Ann Phillips, Lyn Rush,
Jennifer Walters

PRODUCTION
DIRECTOR OF PRODUCTION
Jim Davis
PRODUCTION MANAGER
Hannah Lobb
TECHNICAL MANAGER
Geoff Farmer
SENIOR TECHNICIAN
(STAGE) Nick Samuel
TECHNICIANS (STAGE)
Paul Adams, Angel Hasted
SENIOR TECHNICIAN
(LIGHTING AND SOUND)
Chris Skinner
TECHNICIANS (LIGHTING
AND SOUND) David Powell,
Neil Queripel, Nathan
Stewart, Matthew Williams,
Neil Williams
TECHNICAL APPRENTICES
James Davison,
Joe McDermott
WARDROBE MANAGER
Deborah Knight
WARDROBE CUTTERS
Emma Aldridge,
Michal Shyne
WARDROBE ASSISTANT
Alison Hartnell
COSTUME MAINTENANCE
Amber Davies, Karen Jones
WORKSHOP MANAGER
Steve Eccleson
WORKSHOP ASSISTANTS
Dave Davies, Andy Sutters
PROPS MAKER Bob Heaton
SCENIC ARTIST Mike Jones

OPERATIONS
DIRECTOR OF OPERATIONS
Andrew Roberts
DUTY FRONT OF HOUSE
MANAGERS Laura Gray,
Gwennan Henstock
OPERATIONS
COORDINATOR Andy Reilly
OPERATIONS
ADMINISTRATOR
Sarah Eldridge
EVENTS COORDINATOR
Nathan Stewart
CHEF Richard Hughes
SOUS CHEF Tina Lane
FOOD & DRINK SUPERVISOR
Salvatore Vena
OPERATIONS TEAM LEADER
Callum Roberts
BAR ASSISTANTS Carol
Williams, Andrew Walls,
Matthew Wright, Delyth
Williams, Daryl Batchelor,
Gwennan Henstock,
Andrew Hughes, Stewart
.Hazledoen
CATERING ASSISTANTS
Rachel Wilday, Ann Phillips,
Callum Selvester, Callum
Roberts, Dave Humphreys,
Kim Holsgrove, Rhiannon
Isaac, Kizi Lane, Enya
Maguire, Jana Fabianova
MERCHANDISE ASSISTANTS
Luisa Sciarillo, Carol
Williams, Delyth Williams
CINEMA CO-ORDINATOR
Mike Roberts
PROJECTIONISTS
Sam Davidson,
Matthew Wright
BUILDING SERVICES
COORDINATOR Jim Scarratt
GREEN ROOM Clare Brown,
Carol Ann Jones,
Caroline Jones
AUDIO DESCRIBERS
Trevor Dennis,
Margaret Jones, Jon Payne,
Diana Stebbing

DEVELOPMENT
DIRECTOR OF
DEVELOPMENT
Daniel Porter-Jones
SPONSORSHIP MANAGER
Annie Dayson

Orange
Tree
Theatre

At its home in Richmond, South West London, the **Orange Tree Theatre** aims
to entertain, challenge, move and amaze with a bold and continually
evolving mix of new and rediscovered plays in our unique in-the-round
space. We want to change lives by telling remarkable stories from a wide
variety of times and places, filtered through the singular imagination of our
writers and the remarkable close-up presence of our actors.

Over its forty-five-year history the Orange Tree has had an exceptional track
record in discovering writers and promoting their early work, as well as
rediscovering artists from the past whose work had either been disregarded
or forgotten.

In the last two years, the OT has been recognised for its work with sixteen
major industry awards, including ten Offies (Off West End Awards), three UK
Theatre Awards, the Alfred Fagon Audience Award and the Peter Brook Empty
Space Award.

In 2016 the Orange Tree's work was seen in twenty-four other towns and
cities across the country.

The OT is proud to be co-producing *Black Mountain* by Brad Birch, *Out of Love*
by Elinor Cook and *How To Be a Kid* by Sarah McDonald-Hughes in the
Roundabout season with Paines Plough and Theatr Clwyd. In Edinburgh, the
OT's co-production with Farnham Maltings of *Jess and Joe Forever* by Zoe
Cooper is at the Traverse Theatre.

The Orange Tree is a registered charity (no. 266128) whose mission is to
enable audiences to experience the next generation of theatre talent,
experiment with ground-breaking new drama and explore the plays of the
past the have inspired the theatremakers of the present. To find out how you
can help us to do that you can visit **orangetreetheatre.co.uk/discover**

Generously supported by the London Borough of Richmond upon Thames.

orangetreetheatre.co.uk | @OrangeTreeThtr | Facebook/Instagram:
OrangeTreeTheatre

Artistic Director	Paul Miller
Executive Director	Sarah Nicholson
Development Director	Alex Jones
Technical Manager	Stuart Burgess
Education Director	Imogen Bond
Theatre Manager	Nicola Courtenay
Finance Manager	Caroline Goodwin
General Manager	Rebecca Murphy
Press & Marketing Manager	Ben Clare
Development Manager	Rebecca Frater
Literary Associate	Guy Jones
Production Technician	Lisa Berrystone
Development Officer	Emma Kendall
Education and Participation Assistant	Izzy Cotterill

AT THE ORANGE TREE THEATRE

7 SEPTEMBER – 7 OCTOBER 2017
An Orange Tree Theatre production in association with Up in Arms
The March on Russia
By David Storey

10 – 28 OCTOBER 2017
A Paines Plough and Pentabus Theatre Company production
Every Brilliant Thing
By Duncan Macmillan with Jonny Donahoe

2 NOVEMBER–2 DECEMBER 2017
An Orange Tree Theatre production
Poison
By Lot Vekemans
Translated by Rina Vergano

7 DEC 2017–20 JAN 2018
An Orange Tree Theatre production
Misalliance
By Bernard Shaw

20 DEC 2017–6 JAN 2018
A Wizard Presents, Orange Tree Theatre and Little Angel Theatre
co-production
Kika's Birthday
By Danyah and John Miller

OUT OF LOVE

Elinor Cook

For Tom

Acknowledgements

Huge thanks to George Perrin, Francesca Moody and all the wonderful people at Paines Plough; Hasan Dixon, Katie Elin-Salt and Sally Messham for bringing my characters so thrillingly to life; Paul Miller and Guy Jones at the Orange Tree Theatre and Tamara Harvey at Theatr Clwyd for their excellent steers and encouragement; Fay Davies and Tumi Belo at the Agency for their support, both creative and practical; Alice Stevenson for setting me writing exercises when I was stuck; Livi Shean for a much-needed holiday; and especially to James Grieve, for directing the play with such detail, sensitivity and understanding.

E.C.

'Even if we're constantly tempted to lower our guard – out of love, or weariness, or sympathy or kindness – we women shouldn't do it. We can lose from one moment to the next everything that we have achieved'

Elena Ferrante,
from an interview in *The New York Times*,
9th December 2014

'Little girls are cute and small only to adults. To one another they are not cute. They are life sized'

Cat's Eye
by Margaret Atwood

'Statistics and newspapers tell me I am unhappy and dying, that I need man and child to fulfil me, that I'm more likely to get breast cancer. And it's biology, it's my own fault, it's divine punishment of the unruly'

'The Battle is Over' by Jenny Hval,
from the album *Apocalypse, Girl*

4

Characters

Actor 1 (*f*):
GRACE / RUTH

Actor 2 (*f*):
LORNA / PENNY

Actor 3 (*m*):
GEORGE / LEONARD / CHARLIE / DAD / MIKE / TED /
CHRISTOPHER / SAM / BOY

This text went to press before the end of rehearsals and so may differ slightly from the play as performed.

1

A scrub of land in a town in the North East of England.

LORNA *is scratching her head vigorously.*

GRACE   Stop scratching.

            LORNA snatches her hand away.

            GRACE turns away for a moment.

            Furtively, LORNA *scratches her head again.*

            I saw that.

LORNA   Sorry.

GRACE   It makes it worse.

            LORNA *folds her hand in her lap.*

            She drums her feet on the ground.

LORNA   Argh but it's so itchy!

GRACE   Here.

            GRACE *takes* LORNA*'s hands.*

            She sits on them.

            Now you can't.

            LORNA *breathes deeply.*

            GRACE *peers at* LORNA*'s head.*

            I can see them.

LORNA   What?

GRACE   On your head.

LORNA   No you can't.

GRACE   Look.

          GRACE *leans over and plucks something from*
          LORNA*'s scalp.*

          There.
          See?

          LORNA *looks.*

          It's alright.
          I've got them as well.

          GRACE *extracts something from her scalp.*

          Here.   ·

          They look at it together.

          They eat our blood.
          Look.
          When I squash him…

LORNA   Don't.

GRACE   That's my blood coming out.
          I love blood.
          Do you dare me to eat it?

          GEORGE *enters.*

          He looks at the girls warily.

GEORGE   Have you still got them?

GRACE   What?

GEORGE   I can't play with you if you've still got them.

GRACE   You've got them too.

GEORGE   No I don't.

GRACE   All the kids in the cottages have got them.

LORNA   Hello George.

          LORNA *gives* GEORGE *a winning smile.*

GEORGE   Alright, Lorna.

GRACE *looks at* GEORGE *and* LORNA.

GRACE   Shall we play weddings?

GEORGE   Not again.

LORNA   Yes.

GEORGE   Alright.

GRACE   Which one of us today?

GEORGE   Lorna.

GRACE   That's not allowed.
            You married her last time.

LORNA   It is allowed.

GRACE   Alright then.
            But get to the good bit.

GEORGE *approaches* LORNA.

LORNA *holds her breath*.

GEORGE *is about to lean in and kiss her.*

You have to do it with your tongue.

GEORGE   What?

LORNA   Grace.

GRACE   That's the proper way.

LORNA *and* GEORGE *look at* GRACE.

They look at each other.

GEORGE *sticks out his tongue*.

LORNA *looks at* GRACE.

GRACE *nods*.

LORNA *sticks out her tongue*.

LORNA *and* GEORGE *lick one another's tongues
experimentally.*

They break away.

Now take your knickers off.

LORNA   No.

GRACE   That's what happens at the end of a wedding.

LORNA   But...

GRACE   Go on.
Do it.

Miserably, LORNA *removes her knickers.*

GEORGE *and* LORNA *look at* GRACE, *awaiting further instructions.*

Now you look like your mum.

LORNA   No I don't.

GRACE   She's running around without any knickers on.
That's why they're getting a divorce.

LORNA   They aren't.

GRACE   Where are you going?

LORNA   Home.

GRACE   Tell George you're sorry.
Then you can go.

LORNA   I won't.

GRACE   Go on.
Tell him.

LORNA   I'm sorry.

GRACE   And you give her a slap.

GEORGE   No...

GRACE   Yes.

He slaps LORNA *gently on the face.*

No not there.
On her bum.

GEORGE   But –

GRACE   Go on.

            GEORGE *slaps* LORNA *on her bum*.

            And again.

            GEORGE *slaps* LORNA *on her bum again*.

LORNA   Ow.

GRACE   Tell her you won't take her back.

GEORGE   I won't take you back.

GRACE   You've had your chance.

GEORGE   You've had your chance.

GRACE   You dirty slut.

GEORGE   You dirty slut.

            LORNA *breaks away from the game*.

            She pulls her knickers back on.

GRACE   Oh it's only a game, Lorna!

            GEORGE *and* GRACE *look at* LORNA, *worried*.

            You still want to be my friend, don't you?
            Don't you?

            LORNA *exits*.

            GRACE *looks at* GEORGE.

            I didn't mean it.
            Is she upset with me?

GEORGE   Girls are always upset.

GRACE   You can marry me now, if you like?

GEORGE   I don't want to.
            I want to play Subbuteo.

            GEORGE *exits*.

2

A small meeting room in a publisher's office.

London.

LORNA   Yes.
            I suppose I've always been interested in unheard
            voices.
            I suppose that's why I'm so keen to work here.

LEONARD   I see.

LORNA   I'm most interested in the stories we don't hear.
            The ones without any glamour or heroism.
            When I was a teenager I took a tape recorder and
            knocked on all the doors in the neighbourhood.
            Asked to speak to the women.
            Mothers, grandmothers, widows.
            Women who'd lived through the war.
            They'd seen so many changes.
            They'd seen their husbands lose their jobs because
            of the mines closing, the shipyards.
            They seemed amazed that someone wanted to ask
            them about it.

LEONARD   How fascinating.

LORNA   I had trouble getting them to open up, at first.
            But once they started they wouldn't stop.

LEONARD   What an enterprising girl.

LORNA   You see, it was really this incredibly emasculated
            society.
            Looking back.
            That's certainly true of my father...
            And then all these fierce, frustrated women.
            Just getting on with it.
            I had tapes and tapes worth of stuff.

LEONARD   Perhaps you should send them to me.
            We could have a listen here.

LORNA   Yes.
           Yes I'll try and dig them out.

LEONARD   And what about school?
           Did you enjoy it?

LORNA   I went to a big noisy comprehensive.
           The boys showing off in front of the girls.
           It was hard to make yourself heard.

LEONARD   But you managed.

LORNA   I was lucky.
           I had a stepfather who really pushed me.
           So I kept my head above water, somehow.
           I was very determined.

LEONARD   Yes I can see that.

LORNA   I made a decision, I think.
           I could either laze about and smoke and drink and
           aspire to nothing.
           Or I could focus.
           Be rigorous.
           I really didn't want to be hemmed in.

LEONARD   I can't imagine anyone hemming you in.
           You strike me as a very ambitious young woman.

           Pause.

           Well, Lorna.
           It's a measly salary, I'm afraid.

LORNA   Yes.

LEONARD   You'll survive?
           London's hellish if you can't make the rent.

LORNA   I'm alright for the time being.
           I'm staying with a friend...

LEONARD   Aha.
           A boyfriend.

LORNA   Um.

LEONARD	I can be quite demanding. I've a temper on me. I have been known to fling manuscripts at my assistants in the past.
LORNA	That won't faze me.
LEONARD	Lots of boring admin work. Fetching my lunch. Ordering taxis. Opening the post.
LORNA	Yes. Yes I assumed.
LEONARD	We've got a few more people to see, of course.
LORNA	Of course.
LEONARD	But I have a feeling we may be seeing more of each other.
LORNA	Yes.
LEONARD	I'll get Samantha to drop you a line.
LORNA	Yes, how wonderful –
LEONARD	I'll see you out. And well done. You can phone your father and tell him you stole the show.
LORNA	My father's dead actually. My real father. He died when I was sixteen.
LEONARD	You've had quite the life, haven't you?
LORNA	I – I think I'm pretty ordinary.
LEONARD	Perhaps it explains why you don't meet my eye.
LORNA	I'm sorry?
LEONARD	You're afraid to reveal too much of yourself.

LORNA	I, I don't know if I am.
LEONARD	Is this your coat? Isn't it smart?
LORNA	Yes –
LEONARD	It's about really owning that confidence. Not just parroting it.
LORNA	Um.
LEONARD	Now. I suggest you head straight to the National Gallery. Look at the medieval tapestries. It's by far the most peaceful spot. Then treat yourself to a glass of wine in the café. It's important to mark the moments when you've excelled.

3

LORNA*'s living room.*

GRACE	This is boring. Are you nearly finished?
LORNA	No.
GRACE	Can we play The Game of Life in a bit?
LORNA	It's packed already.
GRACE	We could get it out. Is it in here?
LORNA	Don't touch that!
GRACE	Why not?
LORNA	It's all Christopher's books and stuff.

GRACE	'*Gender, Sex and Sexuality*'. Eurgh.
LORNA	Put it back.
GRACE	Is your stepfather a sex perv?
LORNA	Shhhh he's only upstairs!
GRACE	'Feminine/masculine, male/female, boy/girl.'
LORNA	Don't read it.
GRACE	'Terms of sexual and gender division like these permeate the way we think and talk about ourselves and each other.' What?
LORNA	Put it down.
GRACE	This is alright actually.
LORNA	Grace –
GRACE	He won't notice if I borrow it.
LORNA	Yes he will.
GRACE	I'll sneak it back. When you're in your new house. It'll be weird not having you next door any more. Do you know who's moving here after you?
LORNA	No.
GRACE	I bet they'll be awful. I bet they'll be four boys called Dave, Dan, Duncan and Derrick. Can I come over later and use the jacuzzi?
LORNA	Well, Christopher wants… He wants us to have a meal. Just as a family.
GRACE	Tomorrow then.
LORNA	It's not exactly a jacuzzi.

GRACE   You said it was.

LORNA   It's just a normal bath.
With these kind of nozzles.
Look, I'll come round to yours or something.

GRACE   I want to see your new room though.

LORNA   It's not that great.

GRACE   You'll have a double bed!

LORNA   Can I still sleep at yours sometimes?

GRACE   Course.

LORNA   Like, when you...
When you make me a nest.

GRACE   With the bean bags.

LORNA   With the cereal crusted on them.

GRACE   My mum washed that off.
But Misty can still join in.
All smelly and delicious.

LORNA   I wish I could have a dog.
Christopher's allergic.

GRACE   I saw your real dad the other day.

LORNA   What?

GRACE   In the Spar.
He bought me a Kinder Egg.

Pause.

LORNA   Did... did he say anything?

GRACE   He said he was off to play football with some
friends after.
But he wasn't wearing football kit.
So I don't know if he was.

Pause.

LORNA   Did… did he say anything about me?

GRACE   Well.
           No.

           Pause.

           Sorry.

LORNA   Doesn't matter.

GRACE   He probably wanted to.

LORNA   What was he buying?

GRACE   What?

LORNA   In the Spar?

           Pause.

GRACE   Oh nothing much.
           Some plasters.
           Toothpaste.

LORNA   What kind?

GRACE   Aquafresh.

LORNA   Anything else?

GRACE   Nope.
           Nothing.

           Pause.

           Do you want to borrow my Whitney Houston
           tape?
           To play in your room tonight.
           If you feel homesick.

LORNA   No it's okay.

GRACE   You can.
           I don't mind.

LORNA   Can I –
           Can I have Take That as well?

GRACE   Um.

            Pause.

            Yes but please be very, very careful with it.

 # 4

A bus stop.

LORNA and GRACE are trying not to look at CHARLIE, who is reading On the Road *by Jack Kerouac.*

They look at him.

He looks up too.

They look away and snort with laughter.

CHARLIE *returns to his book.*

GRACE *and* LORNA *smirk.*

CHARLIE *looks up.*

CHARLIE   You two aren't at St Margaret's are you?

            GRACE *and* LORNA *explode into laughter.*

GRACE   Chuh!
            No.

LORNA   St Margaret's!
            As if!

CHARLIE   I didn't think you were.
            We had a social with them last week.
            I would have seen you.

LORNA   What's a social?

CHARLIE   You know.
            Like a dance.
            A disco.

GRACE *scoffs*.

Are you waiting for the forty-three?
That goes near St Agatha's.

GRACE   The forty-three is the toff bus.

LORNA   We don't go to St Agatha's.

GRACE   Stupid.

LORNA   We're at Thornfields.

CHARLIE   The comp?
          I actually really nearly went to the comp.

LORNA   Did you?

GRACE   Yeah right.

CHARLIE   My parents are socialists, really.
          But I ended up getting a scholarship to St Luke's.

GRACE   Big whoop.

CHARLIE   I wish I hadn't though.
          It's horrible at my school.

LORNA   Why?

CHARLIE   Oh it's just this little bubble.
          I bet there are loads of interesting people at
          Thornfields.
          I bet people are so much more connected.

GRACE   Connected to what?

CHARLIE   Oh, you know.
          To their roots.
          Because their families are rooted in these great
          industries.
          The ships, the mines.

GRACE   Well, they're all gone now.

LORNA   Grace's dad worked in the mines.

GRACE   So did yours.

CHARLIE   Did they?
            Gosh that's so interesting.
            I'd love to talk to them for a project I'm doing.
            Could I do that?

GRACE   Why?

CHARLIE   I just, I think it's so important.
            To communicate.
            To reach a better understanding.
            I hate all these divisions so much.

LORNA   Yes.

CHARLIE   I want to be a journalist, you see.
            I'm just really interested in people.
            I'm applying to do this media and
            communications course at Goldsmiths.
            That's in London.
            Have you been to London?

LORNA   Yes.

GRACE   She's only been once.

CHARLIE   I think it's my favourite place in the whole world.

LORNA   Me too.

GRACE   You do not.
            That crazy man was humping a lamp post.
            That's all you talked about.

CHARLIE   What university do you want to go to?

GRACE   We're only thirteen.

CHARLIE   Really?
            You look older.

            His eyes dart to LORNA*'s chest for a moment.*

            *She folds her arms self-consciously across her
            chest.*

LORNA   My stepdad teaches at the university here.
            I don't really know about any others…

GRACE   I'm going to go to one.

LORNA   Are you?

GRACE   Of course I am.

LORNA   You never said.

GRACE   Yes I have.
        I've always wanted to.

LORNA   Well, so have I.

GRACE   (*To* CHARLIE.) What are you reading anyway?

CHARLIE (*Replying to* LORNA.) Oh God, sorry, it's such
        a cliché.
        On the Road by Jack Kerouac.
        It's practically handed out on prescription if
        you're a man.

GRACE   What about if you're a woman?

CHARLIE (*To* LORNA.) I'm Charlie, by the way.

LORNA   Oh um.
        Lorna.

CHARLIE (*To* LORNA.) We're having another social at my
        school in a few weeks, so…
        If you wanted.
        Well, you should come.

        LORNA *looks at* GRACE, *confused.*

        (*To* LORNA.) I mean, it's up to you.
        If you're not too busy.

GRACE   Here comes the toff bus.

CHARLIE It'll probably be really lame but well.
        Let me know.
        I really like your hair.
        Your hairstyle.

LORNA   Do you?

GRACE	Don't be late for rugger now, Charlie!
	CHARLIE *exits*.
	Did you notice how he didn't ask us anything about ourselves?
LORNA	Yes he did.
GRACE	What?
LORNA	Did I like London. Did I want to go to the dance.
GRACE	Interview our dads! Can you imagine him in the same room as my dad?
LORNA	I'm not going to go though. I don't think. No I don't think I am.
GRACE	It's a good idea though… I'll give him that. Though I bet he wouldn't speak to a single woman.
LORNA	Although I could I suppose. But what would I wear?
GRACE	They wouldn't speak to him anyway. The women. But they'd speak to me. Don't you think? I'm going to ask them questions. No one ever asks them anything.
LORNA	But what if he changes his mind? He'd be better off going with a St Agatha's girl. What's he see in me, anyway?
GRACE	I bet they'd tell me all kinds of wicked stuff.
LORNA	He was quite nice though, wasn't he?
GRACE	Who? Oh.
LORNA	Didn't you think he was nice?

GRACE   He's too old for you.

LORNA   He had ever such a nice voice.
          Didn't you think?

GRACE   Oh my God.

LORNA   What?

GRACE   You like posh boys.

LORNA   I do not.

GRACE   I don't know why I'm surprised.

5

GRACE*'s kitchen.*

A baby crying.

DAD *enters.*

DAD   Grace.
          You have to stop her crying.

          Silence.

          Your mother's trying to sleep.
          Grace.

          GRACE *wraps her arms around her knees and
          puts her head on them.*

          Look, give her here.

          Pause.

          Alright then.

          Pause.

          There we go.
          What's all this fuss about then?

What's all this silly fuss?
Oh, Grace, it's just her nappy.

Pause.

Well now.
There we are.
This isn't so bad is it, Martha?
You and your old granddad, eh?
Hey, this takes me back, Grace.
Grace...?

Silence.

Lorna's back from that college for a few weeks.
Why don't you pop round with – ?

GRACE   No.

Pause.

Give her here.

DAD   She's settling now.

GRACE   Give her to me.

Pause.

She looks nothing like me.

DAD   The spit of you.

GRACE   I don't see it.
I don't see anything I recognise.

Pause.

At least I don't see him.
At least there's that.
Why is Mum sleeping?

DAD   You know why.
Only got back from the hospital few hours ago.

GRACE   Don't think she's been in the same room as me
for days.

DAD   Why do you think she's working so hard?
           Who's that for?

GRACE   She's not obliged to love me.
           Neither of you are.

DAD   Don't start with that.

GRACE   You didn't pick me.
           You just ended up with me.
           Anyone who says anything else is a liar.

           Pause.

DAD   She looks like your grandma.
           My mum.
           I reckon.

GRACE   I don't remember her that well.

DAD   You've always reminded me of her.

GRACE   In what way?

DAD   She had a lovely singing voice.

GRACE   I can't sing a note.

DAD   I know.

GRACE   So what are you talking about?

           DAD *laughs.*

           Then he starts to cough.

           He coughs for a while.

           GRACE *watches him.*

           He controls himself eventually.

           Can I get you anything?

DAD   No, love.

GRACE   No but –
           Sorry.
           How's your chest and everything?

DAD   You're alright.

GRACE   What do you fancy to eat?
           I'll take her with me to the shops and –

DAD   Ted's been.

GRACE   Ted has?

DAD   You keep warm in here.

GRACE   I meant to go but the time just –
           I just kept sitting.

DAD   You're alright.

GRACE   Don't keep saying that.

DAD   Ted's been, it's alright –

GRACE   It wasn't alright last week.
           Was it?

DAD   You what?

GRACE   Stop pretending.

DAD   What?

GRACE   Stop pretending to be nice.

           Pause.

           She's sleeping.
           When she sleeps, I sleep.

DAD   Grace –

GRACE   Close the door on your way out.

6

A church.

GRACE *and* MIKE *are are sat together.*

LORNA *is sitting a little separately from them, alone.*

GRACE *and* MIKE *speak in hushed voices.*

MIKE	I hate churches.
GRACE	Shh.
MIKE	Really fucking hate them.
GRACE	Alright don't go on about it.
	Pause.
MIKE	You look good in black.
GRACE	I hate this skirt. I feel like a waitress.
MIKE	You should wear black more often.
GRACE	I did my nails too. Look. Proper Goth.
	He kisses her fingers.
	I'll paint yours later if you want.
MIKE	Yeah go on then.
GRACE	Do your eyes as well.
MIKE	Yeah?
GRACE	Reckon you'd look good with eyeliner.
MIKE	Is that my shirt?
GRACE	Yeah.
MIKE	Thief.

GRACE   I smell just like you.
          God.
          Look at her…

          They look at LORNA.

          Has she seen us?

MIKE   Dunno.

GRACE   I should go over.

MIKE   Suit yourself.

GRACE   I should.
          I should.

MIKE   Not a lot you can say, is there?

GRACE   Doesn't she look beautiful?

MIKE   The coffin's coming.

GRACE   Oh fuck.

          GRACE *squeezes her eyes tightly shut.*

          She takes MIKE's *hand.*

          He squeezes it.

          LORNA *sits up a little straighter, alert.*

          Has it gone past?

MIKE   Yeah.
          At the front now.

          Pause.

GRACE   What a selfish, shitty, shit thing to do.

MIKE   Poor bloke.

GRACE   She won't get angry.
          She's crap at getting angry.

MIKE   How'd he do it?

GRACE   Don't ask me that.

MIKE   Pills, was it?
            Dressing-gown cord?

GRACE   I said, don't.

            Pause.

            Have you ever felt that?
            Like you wanted to do that?

MIKE   No.
            But I wouldn't blame someone for wanting to.

GRACE   If you ever die, I'll kill you.

MIKE   Alright then.

GRACE   You better fucking promise.

MIKE   I promise.

GRACE   Mike.

MIKE   What?

GRACE   Remember in juniors.
            When you'd put your hand under my skirt.

MIKE   Never did that.

GRACE   I used to pretend I didn't like it.

            She takes his hand and puts it under her skirt.

            A moment.

            That's good.

MIKE   Yeah?

GRACE   Yeah.
            Just let me –

            She shifts a bit.

            Okay yes.
            Oh fuck yes.

            LORNA *turns around.*

She sees GRACE *and* MIKE.

She sees MIKE'*s hand under* GRACE'*s skirt.*

LORNA *and* GRACE *stare at each other for a moment.*

Mike move your fucking hand.

MIKE   Jesus...

LORNA *stands up and starts to go, her head down.*

Where's she going?
It's her dad's funeral, isn't it?

GRACE   Lorna, wait –

LORNA *exits.*

7

Outside the school gates.

DAD   Lorna?

LORNA   Oh, God.

DAD   Lorna, sweetheart?

GRACE   That's never your dad, is it?

LORNA   Just keep walking.

DAD   Hang on a second there, love – !

LORNA   (*To* GRACE.) Don't keep staring.

DAD   There's my favourite girl.
                Well now, you've shot up, haven't you?!

LORNA   I, I didn't see you.

GRACE   Why aren't you wearing a coat, Mr Lorimer?

DAD	Is that Grace Peterson?
GRACE	Course it is!
DAD	Aren't you growing up so gorgeous?
LORNA	Dad, what are you doing here? You're freezing.
GRACE	Gorgeous? Am I?
DAD	Read any good books lately, Gracie? Always had your nose in a book.
GRACE	*Jane Eyre*. She's very plain. Not like me, I'm *gorgeous*!
DAD	Hey, you hungry? Could get a nice tea together. That place does the jam tarts. Or I thought I'd take you for a drive.
LORNA	I can't right now.
DAD	Aw come on, pet. I've got my licence again.
LORNA	We're doing homework.
GRACE	I don't mind going for a drive.
DAD	There you go, see! I'll take you to the seaside. Buy you both an ice cream.
GRACE	Can we get fish and chips first?
DAD	Now hang on a minute. I got something for you, love.
LORNA	Please, Dad.
DAD	The lass in the shop said this was probably right.
GRACE	Ooh, lessee!

LORNA   Grace.

DAD   Hold it up, come on.

LORNA   Dad, no.

DAD   She said it was their most popular frock.
           Flying off the rack, she said.

GRACE   C&A?

DAD   Bobby dazzler, isn't it?

LORNA   This... this is for a kid.
           A little kid.

GRACE   Look!
           Does it suit me?

DAD   I, I thought it was about right.
           What are you now, nine, ten?

GRACE   We're ten!
           Fancy forgetting that!

LORNA   And it's –
           It's cheap.

DAD   Well now...
           The lass in the shop...

LORNA   I hate that shop.
           It's horrible and, and –
           Tacky.

GRACE   Christopher buys all her clothes from France.
           All these weird shirts with collars.

DAD   You used to have one just like it.
           Wore it on your birthdays.
           Put your hair in those bunches.

LORNA   That was years and years and years ago!

DAD   So you don't like it?

GRACE   *I* like it.

DAD
Whoops!
Another black mark.
What am I on now then, Lorna?
How many strikes, eh?

Pause.

Look.
What you doing next weekend?
We'll go to the shopping centre together.
Pick out something you like the look of.
Two things.
Milkshake at McDonald's after.

LORNA
I –
I can't.

DAD
Been ages since we've spent the weekend
together, eh?

LORNA
I do gymnastics on Saturdays.

GRACE
She's really good.
She can do an Arab Spring.

LORNA
Well, and other things.
Arab Springs are quite easy.

GRACE
Look, I can do one too.
Look.

DAD
I don't really understand what you're punishing
me for, pet.

Silence.

LORNA
Come on, Grace.

DAD
Anyone would think –
Ha!
Anyone would think I was the one who left!

LORNA
Dad, don't.

DAD
I've been improving myself, Lorna.
Been taking classes at the community centre.

I joined the library and I read a book a week.
Hear that, Grace?

GRACE   Yes.

DAD   (*To* LORNA.) Will you tell your mother?
That I've been reading books and learning
fucking, fucking furniture upholstery.
Will you do that for me?

LORNA   I, I can't, Dad, she won't...

DAD   Oh, look, don't get upset, pet.
I'm sorry.
Putting you in the middle of it all.
Wrong again.
Sorry.

LORNA   Stop that!

DAD   What?

LORNA   Stop apologising all the time!

DAD   Sorry.

LORNA   It's no wonder she left you.

Silence.

DAD   Right then.
Give you a ring in a few weeks.
If I've time.

LORNA   I'll come to the shopping centre with you.
I will.

DAD   No you're alright.

LORNA   Dad –

DAD   Don't want to take ungrateful girls for treats.

LORNA   Please.
I really want to.
Dad?

DAD *exits.*

GRACE	Well if you don't want the dress, I'll have it –
LORNA	No.
GRACE	You don't have to snatch.

 # 8

A street.

LORNA	Grace?
GRACE	What.
LORNA	Were you just going to walk past me?
GRACE	No.

They look at each other.

Unsure what to say.

| LORNA | I'm only back for a bit.
Mum and Christopher are splitting up. |
| GRACE | I know.
Martha, stop it.
Stop it. |
| LORNA | I can't believe she's –
I can't believe you made her. |

Silence.

GRACE	Come round later.
LORNA	Really?
GRACE	If you like.
LORNA	Yes.
It's just –
I was planning to get the train back to…
You see, I've got a date –

GRACE	Don't then.
LORNA	No, I'll stay. I'll cancel the –
GRACE	Don't bother.
LORNA	Grace, wait –

GRACE *exits*.

9

A basement club.

Music.

LORNA *and* TED.

TED	So where's my sister then?
LORNA	With Mike somewhere. Some dark corner.
TED	Have you heard the state of his band?
LORNA	She's mad about him.
TED	What about your bloke. What's his name again? Charlie?
LORNA	Charlie was ages ago. I'm with Cameron now.
TED	Cameron, course it is. He not around tonight?
LORNA	No he's up in Edinburgh still. Uni mates.
TED	That's a shame. Miss seeing in the new century together.

LORNA   Do you want to dance, Ted?

Pause.

TED   Yeah alright.

LORNA   No not like that.

TED   How then?

LORNA   Just, put your arms round me and…
There.
That's it.

TED   Now what?

LORNA   Come a bit closer.

TED   Like that.

LORNA   Yeah.
That's good.

They look at each other.

I've never seen you this close up before.

TED   What you reckon?

LORNA   You look like Grace.

TED   Except I got the good looks.

LORNA   Your eyes are green though.

TED   Yours are brown.

LORNA   You're shaking.

TED   Am I?

They dance.

LORNA   I just want this year to be over.
Don't you?

TED   Not right now.

LORNA   I want to pretend it didn't happen.
I want to scrub it out.

TED   Can't do that.

LORNA   You can make yourself forget though.
            I'm getting good at that.

            They look at each other.

            He leans across and kisses her.

            They kiss for a while.

TED   God…

LORNA   No don't stop.

TED   God, Lorna…

LORNA   Ted.
            Don't stop.

TED   You're beautiful, you are.

LORNA   No don't start with all that.
            That's not what I want.

TED   It was nice having you round the house all the
            time when we were kids.

LORNA   Let's go somewhere.
            Let's go somewhere dark and quiet.
            Come on.

TED   I used to sit outside Grace's bedroom and listen to
            the two of you.
            When you were in there it was like everything was
            brighter, or something.
            Better.
            I used to…
            This is really stupid, but…
            I used to think that we'd get married.
            Thought about what dress you'd wear.

LORNA   Have you got your car?

TED   Thought about hiring a camper van and the two of
            us just…
            Leaving, the middle of the night.

We could go up to the lakes.
Sleep in bed and breakfasts and we'd have a dog,
I thought.
Then a kid.
Three kids.
We'd just be on the road all the time and the kids
would have long hair.
You'd be beautiful, in bare feet.
Stupid isn't it?
But it's what I thought…
Ow.
Your nails…

LORNA   Come on.

TED   Let's keep dancing a bit longer.

LORNA   Don't you want me, Ted?

TED   Can't we just… just talk?
             For a while?

LORNA   I don't want to talk.

TED   What you biting me for?

LORNA   Are you really this stupid, Ted?

TED   Hang on –

LORNA   Or are you just a pussy?
             Is that it?

             Pause.

             A camper van.
             The Lakes.
             Who are you kidding?

TED   What?

LORNA   Have you ever been anywhere, Ted?

TED   Yeah.
             Yeah I've been places.

LORNA   Where?

TED   Alright.
Let's see.
Newcastle.
Manchester.
My granddad lives in Sheffield.

LORNA   The giddy heights.

TED   What did you say?

LORNA   Why'd you leave school last year?

TED   Are you having a go at me?

LORNA   Why?

TED   Well cos…
Cos I wanted to get a job.
Help my folks out.

LORNA   And have you got a job?

TED   I'm looking.

LORNA   So, what?
You're signing on?

TED   For the moment, yeah.

LORNA   Got a bit of time on your hands then.

TED   I keep busy.

LORNA   Don't you think you could help your sister out
a bit more?

TED   You what?

LORNA   Don't you think that might be nice?

TED   I help out.

LORNA   How exactly?

TED   I –
I keep my room clean, I…

LORNA   Do you realise how much she does for you?
          Every single day.
          Do you have any idea?

TED   Okay, I should do more.
          I get it.
          I'm sorry.
          Is that what you want me to say?

LORNA   When was the last time you lifted a finger for
          your dad?

TED   Dad's...
          Dad's difficult.
          She's better with him.

LORNA   She holds a jar out for him to spit into.

TED   He loves her.
          He loves her more.

LORNA   She mushes all his food into a paste.
          She helps him to the toilet.

TED   I'd be no good at all of that.

LORNA   God, Ted, you remind me so much of my father.

TED   What?

LORNA   And we all know what happened to him.

          Silence.

TED   I'll go and find Grace.
          Tell her you need a word.

LORNA   Don't bother.
          I don't need any help from your family.

10

Outside GRACE*'s house.*

GRACE   What you doing standing out there?

LORNA   Nothing.

GRACE   It's nearly midnight.

LORNA   I know.

GRACE   Your mum and dad arguing again?

          Pause.

          Come on.

LORNA   What?

GRACE   The window.

LORNA   What if your dad hears?

GRACE   Keep your voice down then.

          LORNA *climbs in the window.*

          Do you want my bed?

LORNA   No.

GRACE   I'll take the bean bag.
          Go on.

LORNA   Will you get in with me?

GRACE   Okay.

          Pause.

LORNA   Your pillow smells nice.

GRACE   Does it?

LORNA   It smells like home.

11

A church hall.

GRACE   You're so thin.

LORNA   Am I?

GRACE   And blonde.

LORNA   It's just…
           Highlights.
           And I was on holiday so…
           Caught the sun a bit.

GRACE   Where did you go?

LORNA   Oh just.
           Just this small seaside resort in Italy.
           You wouldn't have heard of it.
           Probably.

           Pause.

           God, Grace.
           I'm really so sorry about Ted –

GRACE   Where's your boyfriend?

LORNA   Oh he's.
           He's just getting me a drink.

GRACE   What's his name again?

LORNA   Reza.

GRACE   What?

LORNA   His mother's Iranian.

GRACE   He didn't need to wear a suit.

LORNA   Well he…
           Wanted to be respectful.

GRACE   A suit like that doesn't look respectful.

LORNA   He was trying to be nice –

GRACE   It looks offensive.

         Pause.

LORNA   How old's Martha now?
         She must be –

GRACE   She's six.
         You sent her a birthday card.
         With a badge.
         'Six.'

LORNA   So –
         So school and everything –

GRACE   He said he wanted to get out.
         See the world.

LORNA   Who?

GRACE   Ted.

         Pause.

         He said you told him to.

LORNA   I don't think I did –

GRACE   Apparently he had no horizons.
         According to you.

LORNA   What more do you want me to say?

GRACE   And now he's really got no horizons.
         None at all.

         Pause.

LORNA   There's always a new thing to blame me for.
         I can't keep up.

GRACE   You don't have to keep sending her things.

LORNA   I –
         I want to.

GRACE   Dresses and cardigans and hats and…
         I don't let her wear them.

LORNA   Why not?

GRACE   I just put them in a drawer.
          I don't open the letters.

LORNA   I wish you would.
          I've tried to say things –

GRACE   She was so excited to meet you today.

LORNA   You talk about me?

GRACE   But I sent her to the neighbours instead.
          I haven't even told her her uncle's dead.
          He wasn't around that much anyway.
          That's his wife.
          She hates me.
          Women tend to hate me.
          I haven't had sex with anyone since Mike.

LORNA   Oh.

GRACE   Some of the girls from the factory set me up with
          a bloke who apparently 'didn't have a problem'.
          With my situation.
          Which was big of him.
          We messed around in the back of his car for a bit
          but I didn't have the heart for it.
          In the end.
          He had one of those faces where the features are
          all squished up in the middle and there's just this
          expanse of face.
          I counted four grey hairs the other week.
          At the front here.
          I pulled them out and now there are six.
          Count them.

LORNA   I, I don't see them.

GRACE   Maybe I'll be one of those women who's silver
          and dramatic by the time they're thirty.
          Or maybe I'll just fade and go colourless and no
          one will notice if I'm there or not.

LORNA   It –
It must be so hard.
I can't imagine how hard it's –

GRACE   Don't you dare look down on me.

LORNA   I don't.
Grace, I don't.

GRACE   I have to go and help Dad.

LORNA   How is he?
I'd love to say hello to him.

GRACE   Nothing stopping you.
He's been sat a matter of metres away from you all day.

She's gone.

12

A park.

GRACE *and* LORNA *are lying down.*

GRACE   I'd like to be touched.

LORNA   Yeah.

GRACE   No but I mean really…
Really touched.

Silence.

I'd like for someone to just…
Run their hands up the entire length of me.
And for my whole body to just kind of…
Dissolve.

Silence.

Would you lie on top of me?

LORNA *stares at her*.

I don't mean it like that.

LORNA   Good!

GRACE   I just…
Don't you ever just…
Long for that weight, on top of you?

She turns and looks at LORNA.

Have you ever had one?

LORNA   One what?
Oh.

Pause.

I think so.

GRACE   Really?

LORNA   Yeah…

GRACE   With Charlie?

LORNA   Yeah…

GRACE   Or on your own?

Pause.

LORNA   I've never tried.

GRACE   What, never?

LORNA   Guess not.

GRACE   Why?!

LORNA   I don't know.

GRACE   It's not that hard.
You just have to kind of experiment.
You experiment, right…?

LORNA *closes her eyes*.

What do you do with him then?

LORNA   I don't know.
          Things.

GRACE   Like what?

LORNA   I don't know, I kind of...
          Touch it, and stuff.

GRACE   With your hand?

LORNA   Yeah.

GRACE   Or with your mouth?

LORNA   Sometimes.

GRACE   Does he do it back?

LORNA   Sometimes...
          I don't really like it.

          Pause.

          I don't know.
          When I'm with him I just feel...

GRACE   What?

LORNA   Wrong or...
          No.
          Frozen.

GRACE   Like, how?

LORNA   Like, I feel...
          Afraid.

GRACE   Isn't that exciting?
          Someone wanting you...

LORNA   Yes...
          No.
          I just –
          I want to be a kid again.

GRACE   What's it like to be wanted?

LORNA   I want to be ten, at the shopping centre, ice-skating,
          I don't care.

GRACE   No one's ever seen me naked except my mum.
            Ted used to peek sometimes.

LORNA   There's nothing in it, for us, it's only for them.

GRACE   What?

LORNA   That's what I think.

GRACE   Then he's doing it wrong.
            Tell him he's doing it wrong.

LORNA   I don't even *know* what's wrong.
            What's right.
            I don't know anything.
            I wish the whole thing would just –
            Go away.
            I hate it.

GRACE   Wait.
            Is that Mike Schofield?

LORNA   Where?

GRACE   Look.

            They look.

LORNA   I haven't seen him since junior school.

GRACE   Me either.

LORNA   Was he always that tall?

GRACE   He used to put his hand under my skirt in maths.

LORNA   Mine too.

GRACE   Mike.
            MIKE SCHOFIELD.

LORNA   What are you doing?

GRACE   Hey Mike?
            Remember me?
            Come over here and talk to us.

13

School playground.

LORNA *and a* BOY *are smoking furtively and giggling.*

GRACE *enters.*

GRACE   Are you smoking?

LORNA   No.

GRACE   You are.
          You'll get a face like an old trout.
          Your fingers and teeth will go yellow.
          Can I have one?

LORNA   No.

GRACE   Why not?

LORNA   You've got PE.

GRACE   So have you.

LORNA   I'm skiving.

GRACE   I'm skiving as well.

LORNA   I'm going to the garage with Tony.

GRACE   Can I come?

LORNA   Why are you still wearing that T-shirt?

GRACE   Cos it's wicked.

LORNA   No one listens to Kylie and Jason any more.

GRACE   I do.

          LORNA *and the* BOY *laugh together.*

          What's so funny?

LORNA   Tell Mr Patel I've got a headache.

GRACE   I'm not going to see Mr Patel.
          I'm not going to PE.
          I told you.

LORNA   You can bounce a ball back and forth with Fred
          Boyle.

GRACE   Fred Boyle is a spastic.

          BOY *tugs* LORNA *by the hand*.

          You can't leave me here.
          At least give me a cigarette.
          Hey.
          I'll tell Mr Patel you've got your period.
          I'll tell him you got it all down your leg.

          LORNA *and* BOY *exit*.

          GRACE *is left by herself*.

14

GRACE*'s bedroom*.

GRACE *is in bed, her head under the covers*.

LORNA   Grace?

          Nothing.

          Okay.
          I'm leaving a tea here for you.
          And there's some Hobnobs for when you feel
          hungry.

GRACE   No.

LORNA   You have to eat something.

GRACE   I want to die.
          I want to take a gun and blow my brains out.

          Pause.

          Shit.
          Sorry.

LORNA   It's okay.

GRACE   That was a crap thing to say.

LORNA   It's okay.

Pause.

GRACE   I hurt.

LORNA   I know.

GRACE   Like, my God.
The pain.
I can't tell where it is.
Is it in my stomach, or my throat, or my chest?
But also it's in my arms, my legs.
I can feel it in my hair.

LORNA   You won't always feel like this.

GRACE   He was everything.

LORNA   He wasn't.
He was awful to you.

GRACE   I sometimes think –
I'd give up everything just to have him one
more time.
If he said –
Grace.
You mean nothing to me, and this will only
happen once.
But I am going to climb through your bedroom
window and strip off your awful Snoopy pyjamas
and pin your arms to the bed and run my tongue
all over you in that way that makes you shake and
scrape my nails down your back and put my hands
around your neck.
Then I would let him.
I would drop everything.
I would let go of Dad's wheelchair in the middle
of the road, a motorway.
To make sure I was waiting in my bed for the
moment he climbed through the window.

Around your neck?

What?

Nothing.

GRACE How ugly am I, Lorna?
    Will you tell me?

LORNA You're not ugly.
    You're beautiful.

GRACE But I want to be the *most* beautiful.
    The most amazing.
    I want everyone to love me.
    Then I'd never get hurt.

LORNA I think you are the most.

GRACE What if I end up like Veronica Cross-Eyes?

LORNA You won't.

GRACE I keep skirting round her house, you know.
    When I go out with my tape recorder.
    She just sits at the window and you can smell it,
    even with the doors closed.

LORNA You won't end up like her.

GRACE Why don't I just knock?
    I should.
    Ask her everything, figure out how she got there.
    Ugh I'm getting sick of the whole project.

LORNA No, you mustn't.

GRACE Why?
    It's just the same story, over and over again, isn't it?
    'He lost his job, he was angry, he took it out on
    me, I got on with it.'
    'He met another woman, she was younger, she
    was his daughter's best friend, his cousin, his
    niece, I got on with it.'

LORNA Budge up.

GRACE   You're freezing.

LORNA   That's why I'm getting in.

GRACE   Put your arms around me then.

LORNA   Alright.

GRACE   You're like a block of wood.

LORNA   Grace?

GRACE   What?

LORNA   When... when Mike and you...

GRACE   Yeah?

LORNA   Did it make you feel a bit...
         Ashamed?

GRACE   What you on about?

LORNA   Cameron hates it when I...
         He just wants be me to quiet.

GRACE   I couldn't be quiet if I wanted to.
         I'd wake the whole town up if I could.

LORNA   He puts his hand over my mouth sometimes...

GRACE   You can see every single one of my ribs.
         Wow.

LORNA   Put them away.

GRACE   All I want to eat is crisps...

LORNA   When was the last time you had a bath?

GRACE   I hate baths.
         They're the most boring activity known to man.

LORNA   You'll end up like Veronica Cross-Eyes.

GRACE   I like the smell.

LORNA   No one else does.

GRACE   Mike used to sniff me.
         He used to breathe in great whiffs of me.

GRACE *stands up*.

LORNA   Where are you going?

GRACE   Just out.

LORNA   Where?

GRACE   None of your business.

LORNA   Don't.

GRACE   What?

LORNA   You know what happened last time.

GRACE   Yes but I'm calm today.
          I'm rational.

LORNA   You need to stop going over there.

GRACE   But he doesn't understand yet!
          I just need to make him understand!

LORNA   I'm not going to let you be humiliated.
          Again.

GRACE   What?

LORNA   He broke up with you, Grace.
          He dumped you.
          He was shagging that fifteen-year-old the whole
          time you were together.

GRACE   He was not.

LORNA   I can't let you keep banging your head against that
          wall, Grace.
          I can't.

GRACE   What do you know about it?
          You've never felt any real emotion for anyone.

LORNA   That's not true.

GRACE   You're not bothered about Cameron.

LORNA   I am!

GRACE   And anyway.
          No one's ever broken your heart.
          You don't know what it's like.

LORNA   How can you say that?

GRACE   What?
          Oh your dad.
          That's not the same.

          Pause.

LORNA   Fine.
          Go on.
          Run back into his skinny, moth-eaten arms.
          I don't care.
          Be my guest.

GRACE   Does my hair smell of sick?

LORNA   Yes it does.
          And your skin is all dry.

GRACE   Your vagina's all dry.

LORNA   BYE THEN.

GRACE   YES BYE.

15

LORNA*'s bedroom.*

CHRISTOPHER What's that?

LORNA   A dress.

CHRISTOPHER That's not what you're wearing to your party,
              is it?

          Pause.

CHRISTOPHER Oh darling.
              I thought you were going to wear your Topshop
              jeans.
              With the nice cardi.
              The sparkly one.

LORNA   I want to wear this.

CHRISTOPHER Is it Grace's or something?
              Looks a bit skimpy.

              LORNA *folds her hands across her chest.*

LORNA   Okay.
          I'll wear something else.

CHRISTOPHER Well look, obviously if you want to wear that
              then I'm not going to stop you.

LORNA   I look fat.

CHRISTOPHER You don't.

LORNA   Like a big blobbery whale.

CHRISTOPHER Now look here –

LORNA   I wish I was like Grace.

CHRISTOPHER You've got a lovely figure.
              Womanly.

LORNA   Ugh.

CHRISTOPHER You do!

LORNA   Can you go outside, please?
               I'm going to get changed.

CHRISTOPHER   Am I not allowed to give compliments to my
               own daughter?

LORNA   I'm not your daughter.

CHRISTOPHER   Not this battle again.

LORNA   Please can you go outside?
               Christopher?

               The doorbell rings.

CHRISTOPHER   That's annoying.
               People aren't supposed to be turning up for
               another couple of hours.

LORNA   Mum can you get the door?
               MUM?

CHRISTOPHER   Who are we expecting?

LORNA   Grace of course.

CHRISTOPHER   Ah.

LORNA   What?

CHRISTOPHER   You should really have asked, darling.

LORNA   Grace comes round whenever.

CHRISTOPHER   Yes, she certainly does.

LORNA   So what?
               She's my best friend.

CHRISTOPHER   I understand that.
               But it might be healthy to have a few other friends
               as well.

LORNA   GRACE.
               I'M IN MY ROOM.

CHRISTOPHER   For a change of perspective from time to time.

LORNA   CAN YOU BRING A BOWL OF CRISPS?
               THERE'S HULA HOOPS.

CHRISTOPHER I just worry she's got a bit of a possessive
               streak.

LORNA   And I do have other friends.
               My whole class is coming to the party, aren't
               they?

CHRISTOPHER She looks at you like she wants to eat you up
               sometimes.

LORNA   What?

CHRISTOPHER And I just don't want you to get hurt.
               In the long run.
               I think we might limit Grace visits to twice a week.

               GRACE *enters*.

GRACE   You don't have real Hula Hoops.
               Only stupid Sainsbury's own-brand ones.

CHRISTOPHER Those are actually for the party, Grace.

               GRACE *tears open a packet and eats them
               combatively.*

               You can both come down and help with the
               tidying in a bit.

LORNA   Okay.

GRACE   I went through your living room just now.
               It's not even messy.

CHRISTOPHER I'll leave you girls to it.
               And I mean it, Lorna.
               Twice a week.
               You'll thank me for it.

               CHRISTOPHER *exits*.

GRACE   Are you wearing that?

LORNA   No.

GRACE	It's too small for you.
LORNA	I KNOW.
GRACE	Alright, keep your hair on.

She munches crisps.

LORNA	Christopher says you want to eat me up.
GRACE	What?
LORNA	Do you?
GRACE	Well I don't know.

She takes LORNA*'s arm.*

She looks at the wrist.

After a moment she bites it.

Nom-nom.

LORNA	Ow.
GRACE	You taste funny. Have you got your period?
LORNA	What?
GRACE	My mum smells all weird when she's got it. I hope I never get it. Have you got it right now?
LORNA	No.
GRACE	She left some blood on the toilet seat one time. My dad went mental. He said it was disgusting.
LORNA	Close your eyes while I get changed.
GRACE	Alright.

GRACE *doesn't close her eyes.*

16

Evening.

A park.

SAM *and* LORNA *are snogging.*

GRACE *watches them.*

GRACE	Hey Sam?
SAM	What?
GRACE	When's your brother getting here then?
SAM	My brother?
LORNA	Yeah your brother's coming.

She looks hard at SAM.

Isn't he?

SAM	Alright.
LORNA	He'll be here really soon.
GRACE	Will he bring his moped?
LORNA	Probably. Won't he, Sam?
SAM	Sure.

SAM *tries to kiss her again.*

LORNA	Don't. My lips are all chapped.
GRACE	Hey Sam.
SAM	What?
GRACE	Guess who's got a job at the factory? Guess.
SAM	Dunno.
GRACE	Me!

SAM   Okay then.

GRACE   So we'll be best buds.

SAM   Yep.

GRACE   Ted said it's like a meat market.
            He said people are always being caught fucking in
            the toilets.
            Is that true?

SAM   I'm not telling you.

GRACE   Lorna's doing work experience at the *Echo* this
            summer.
            Did you know that?

LORNA   Why do you keep going on about it?

GRACE   Hey Sam.

SAM   What?

GRACE   Look.

LORNA   Grace, fuck off.

GRACE   No but look at me.
            Look.
            Am I being really sexy?
            Is this really sexy dancing?

LORNA   Sit down.

GRACE   What would you give me out of ten, Sam?

SAM   You what?

GRACE   What am I out of ten?
            Go on.

SAM   Nah.

GRACE   Face first.
            Then body.
            That's how you lads do it, isn't it?

SAM   I dunno...

GRACE   Okay then.
            What's Lorna?

LORNA   What?

SAM   Eight.

LORNA   Fuck off.

SAM   Eight's good!

GRACE   No, you're not listening.
            What would you give her for her face?
            And then what would you give her for her body?

LORNA   Can you shut up?

SAM   I dunno, maybe...

LORNA   I don't want to know –

SAM   Like, eight out of ten for body.
            And like, seven out of ten for face.

            LORNA *puts her hands over her ears.*

            But nine out of ten for tits.

            He tries to kiss LORNA *again.*

            She turns her head away.

GRACE   Do you know?
            Now that I come to think about it, Sam Richardson.
            You are like a stone-cold ten out of ten.

SAM   Oh yeah?

GRACE   I mean, let's talk about your mouth.

LORNA   I'm cold.
            I want to go in now.

GRACE   Your mouth is basically depravity itself.
            That gets a ten.

LORNA   Can you lend me your jacket, Sam.
            Sam?

GRACE   And your wrists.
          Just look at them, peeking out of your sleeves.
          I don't know why, but something about that just
          really does it for me.
          Ten.

SAM   What else?

LORNA   Sam.

GRACE   Your neck.
          I'd like to put my face right up close to it.
          Inhale it.
          Your Adam's apple.
          Your shoulders, God, your shoulders.
          Ten, ten, ten.

SAM   You're not so bad yourself.

GRACE   Oh I'm a six.

SAM   I dunno...

GRACE   I'm not sexy like Lorna.
          All the boys want Lorna.

SAM   Oh all the boys, eh?

GRACE   People don't look at me like that.

SAM   Maybe they should.

GRACE   And yet.
          Want to know what the really ironic thing is, Sam?

SAM   What's that?

GRACE   I am absolutely.
          Gagging for it.

          She leans over and kisses SAM *on the mouth.*

          He lets her.

          LORNA *watches, mesmerised and thrown.*

          GRACE *breaks out of the kiss first.*

She claps her hands over her mouth.

You are a bad man, Sam Richardson.

SAM   You started it.

GRACE   Your girlfriend's standing right there.

SAM   We're only messing around.

GRACE   She doesn't want to be your girlfriend any more.

LORNA   Grace, stop it.

GRACE   That was a test.

SAM   What?

GRACE   And you failed it.

SAM   It's not like we're married...

LORNA   I, I think we should just all go home.

GRACE   No.
          I think Sam should go home.

SAM   My shift starts in five minutes anyway.

GRACE   Well then.
          Off you go.

LORNA   No, you don't have to –

GRACE   Yes he does.

SAM   You girls are exhausting.

GRACE   Trot along and think about what you've done.
          That's it.

          SAM *exits.*

          You're welcome.

LORNA   I don't understand you.

GRACE   What?

LORNA   Why are you here?

GRACE   You invited me.
         You told me Sam's brother was coming.

LORNA   Sam's brother looks like Robbie Williams.
         He's going out with Kirsty Flack.
         In what universe would he be here?

GRACE   Why'd you say he would be here then?

LORNA   Why don't you have any other friends?

GRACE   I do.

LORNA   Where are they, Grace?
         Show me where they are.

GRACE   It's not my fault everyone in this town is a dolt.
         Apart from you.

LORNA   You're too much sometimes.

GRACE   You still like me though.
         Don't you?

         Pause.

         Don't you, Lorna?

LORNA   You're not a six out of ten.
         You're more like a five-and-a-half.

17

GRACE*'s house.*

GRACE	Where were you yesterday?
LORNA	What?
GRACE	Did I say you could hold my Barbie?
LORNA	It's only a Sindy. Stop pretending it's a Barbie.
GRACE	I called round for you. You weren't in.
LORNA	Only at the ice rink.
GRACE	Who with?
LORNA	Beth Sutton. Her mum took us.
GRACE	Just Beth Sutton?
LORNA	And Lindsay Drake.
	Pause.
GRACE	She's got eczema.
LORNA	Only on her hands.
GRACE	Her face as well.
LORNA	Only a bit.
GRACE	She flakes everywhere. Was she flaking all over the rink?
LORNA	Beth had a lovely coat.
GRACE	What?
LORNA	It's got a fake-fur hood.
GRACE	She probably stole it.
LORNA	What?
GRACE	Bet she did. Her dad's a thief.

My dad says.
He's brazenly stealing from the good people of
this community.

LORNA   He gives her five pounds a week pocket money.

GRACE   That's a shame.
She'll be spoilt.

Pause.

LORNA   She actually –
She fell over quite a few times.

GRACE   Did she?

LORNA   She was trying to skate backwards.

GRACE   I'm good at that.

LORNA   And she went right into this man.
Who shouted at her.

GRACE   What did her mum say?

LORNA   She wasn't watching.

GRACE   Typical.
Typical.

Pause.

It's okay to have other friends.

LORNA   I know.

GRACE   But you do need to ask me first.
Cos I'm your best friend.

LORNA   Her mum rang my mum.
I didn't know –

GRACE   It's okay just this once.

LORNA   I'm sorry.

GRACE   I know you are.
But next time.
You have to ask.

18

LORNA*'s bedroom.*

LORNA	How many pairs of jeans should I take? What about Woof the Dog? Will I look stupid if I have him on the bed? All my posters are embarrassing. I need some art prints in proper frames, but not Picasso or Matisse cos that's such a cliché. What other artists are there? Have you started packing yet?
GRACE	No.
LORNA	Look at my room, it's a bomb-site. Have you read everything on your reading list? I'm stuck on the first one.
GRACE	Lorna.
LORNA	I just keep reading the same page over and over again and then giving up cos I have to look up every other word and I just can't be bothered.
GRACE	Lorna.
LORNA	What?
GRACE	I went to the doctor.
LORNA	What?
GRACE	He says I'm three months pregnant.
LORNA	No.
GRACE	Yes.
LORNA	But.
GRACE	I'm sorry.
	Pause.
LORNA	I don't understand.
GRACE	Mike.

LORNA	What?
GRACE	(*Louder.*) Mike.
LORNA	No.
GRACE	Don't be angry.
LORNA	Grace, you're leaving next week. We're leaving next week.
GRACE	I can't.
LORNA	You have to.
GRACE	I don't know what to do. Tell me what to do.

Pause.

Please look at me.

LORNA	You can get a pill. Two pills. You just get them from the doctor, I think. And, and it all comes out in the toilet or something. It's easy.
GRACE	It's too late for that.
LORNA	Well then you just get it taken out.
GRACE	It's too late. For anything. I just have to have it.

Pause.

I've been riding my bike everywhere.

LORNA	Why?
GRACE	I thought it might do something.
LORNA	That's stupid, Grace. Why would it do that?
GRACE	I'm cleverer than you.

LORNA   So I'm supposed to just go on my own?
           By myself?

GRACE   I don't know.

LORNA   Was it really worth it?
           For just one last time with him?

GRACE   It wasn't just once.

LORNA   What?

GRACE   We did it loads and loads of times after that and
           I didn't tell you.

           Silence.

           Lorna, look at me.

LORNA   There's something wrong with you.

GRACE   There isn't.

LORNA   Even at my own father's funeral.
           Even then.

GRACE   There's nothing wrong with me.

LORNA   I saw you.
           His hand in your knickers.
           You didn't even look at me.
           You couldn't even tell me you were sorry.

GRACE   I –
           I didn't know what to say.

LORNA   It's like you're obsessed.
           It's not normal.

GRACE   It wasn't about that.
           I was just –

LORNA   And now look what's happened to you.
           You've just escaped one prison.
           Now you're locking yourself in another one.
           Why would you do that?

GRACE   I hate the way you talk about my life.
          Like I'm supposed to be ashamed.

LORNA   You said to me, that night.
          You said, don't let me talk myself out of it.

GRACE   Out of what?

LORNA   All that money.
          In a box under your bed.

GRACE   What money?

LORNA   You told me you were going mad.
          That if you didn't get out now you never would.
          You *said*.

GRACE   I never said that.

LORNA   I could go into your room and find it.
          I could show it to you.
          I could show it to your dad.

GRACE   Don't you dare.

LORNA   So you admit it?

GRACE   At least I'm not trying to be a little girl for the rest
          of my life.

LORNA   What?

GRACE   Listen to you earlier, chattering away like you're
          eleven years old.
          Why are you so frightened of your body, Lorna?
          Why does it disturb you so much?
          Why are you so afraid to let yourself go?
          Cos you're scared of what you'll find?
          Cos you're scared you're like your mother?

LORNA   Shut up.

GRACE   Look at yourself in the mirror.
          Look at yourself and accept what you are.
          That's why all the boys want you.
          Cos they can smell it.

LORNA   Get out of my room.

GRACE   Why do you think Christopher lavishes you with
all that attention?
Why do you think all those men beep their horns
and chase you down the street and try and put
their hands up your skirt?
You know it and I know it.
It doesn't mean you're better.
It just means deep down you're filth.

LORNA   Get out.
Now.

GRACE   This is the best thing that's ever happened to you.
This way you get to sail off, be special.
And I get to stay here, be nothing.
Cos that's what I deserve.
Isn't it?
Cos I *am* nothing.
Isn't that what you think?

LORNA   Of course it isn't.
You're worth so much more than me.
Everybody knows it.

GRACE   Touch me again and I'll kill you.

LORNA   Alright, forget it –

GRACE   Come on, Lorna.
You can do better than that.

LORNA   Ow.

GRACE   You've got teeth and nails, haven't you?
Come on.

LORNA   No.

GRACE   Have you ever seen someone really get the shit
beaten out of them?
Have you?

LORNA   Get off.

GRACE   I have.
         I've seen it again and again.

LORNA   You're pulling it out –

GRACE   Fight back, come on!

LORNA   Stop it.

GRACE   Punch me in the stomach.
         Go on.

LORNA   No.

GRACE   Push me down the stairs.
         Go on.
         Do it.

LORNA   No.

GRACE   DO IT.

LORNA   I would never do that to you.
         You know I wouldn't.

GRACE   Why are you such a pussy?

LORNA   Your dad would though, wouldn't he?

GRACE   What?

LORNA   Except now he can't.
         The old cripple.

GRACE   What did you say?

LORNA   I'm the only person who ever loved you.

GRACE   Shut up.

LORNA   Ted barely sees you.

GRACE   Shut up.

LORNA   Your mum doesn't care.
         Your dad thinks you're his slave.
         Mike left you.

GRACE   You better stop talking right now.

LORNA   I'm the only one.
         The only one who has the patience and the
         fortitude and the sheer fucking stupidity it takes to
         love a person like you, Grace.
         No one else has it in them.
         That baby won't love you and you won't love it.

         GRACE *screams at the top of her lungs.*

         Silence.

Holly — Lorna?

19

GRACE*'s kitchen.*

GRACE   Ta-dah.

LORNA   You cooked this?

GRACE   Yeah.

LORNA   Wow.
         I'm not allowed to touch the cooker at home.

GRACE   I can do spaghetti hoops as well.
         Fish fingers.
         Cheese on toast.

LORNA   Did your mum teach you?

GRACE   No.
         I read a book.

LORNA   Sometimes me and my mum make a cake.
         But they don't turn out that nice.

GRACE   I give Ted his tea most days.
         And Dad too.

LORNA   Your mum's always at the hospital.

GRACE   She's helping people.

LORNA   Is –
           Is your dad around then?

GRACE   He's having a little lie-down.

LORNA   Oh.

GRACE   Are you scared of him?

           Pause.

           It's just the unemployment.
           It's not how he really is.

LORNA   My dad's unemployed.

GRACE   Yeah but your dad's…

LORNA   He never shouts.

GRACE   Your mum does.

LORNA   What?

GRACE   Why's she never come and see my mum any
           more?

LORNA   She does.
           Sometimes.

GRACE   Hardly ever.

LORNA   She's got her job at the university.

GRACE   What's she doing up there?

LORNA   Secretary or something.

GRACE   Sometimes my mum has to put her finger up
           people's bums.

LORNA   You always say that.

DAD   (*Off.*) Grace?
           Grace?

GRACE   Okay you have to go now.

LORNA   But I haven't finished –

GRACE   Hurry, hurry, hurry.

LORNA   Why do I have to – ?

GRACE   I'm serious, Lorna.
           Just go.
           GO.

20

A plush doctor's waiting room.

LORNA   Is that magazine alright for you?

GRACE   It's fine.

LORNA   Mine says October 2011.
           Look.

           Pause.

           Sorry it's taking so long.

GRACE   It's okay.

LORNA   No but.
           The whole point of private is that you don't wait.
           That's the whole point.

GRACE   Things happen.
           Delays.

LORNA   I know you have to get the train.
           Though I wish you'd just stay with us for the night.
           Or longer.
           However long you need.

GRACE   Martha's got her exams.

LORNA   Oh I got a card.
           Hang on.
           Does she still like parrots?

GRACE   She's more in to geology and crystals now.
          She's such a nerd.

LORNA   Oh so this won't – ?

GRACE   No that'll be fine.
          She'll love it.

          Pause.

          What's he like?
          The doctor?

LORNA   He's.
          He's very nice.

GRACE   Yeah?

LORNA   Sense of humour.

GRACE   Good looking?

LORNA   I mean, he's probably sixty-five.

GRACE   Could be confusing.
          A good-looking man rootling around down there.

LORNA   I don't think you'll have any problems.

          Pause.

GRACE   I'll pay you back.
          Somehow, I'll find a way and...

LORNA   No.

GRACE   I will.

LORNA   I don't expect –

GRACE   But it isn't right.
          I can't just take it and not –

LORNA   Yes you can.

GRACE   You worked hard for that money.

LORNA   Yes...

GRACE   I think about you.
         In your fancy office.
         It makes me happy.

         Pause.

LORNA   I'm still only...
         I'm only Assistant Editor.

GRACE   Seems like you're the only person who has any
         actual ideas there.
         Sure you'll get promoted soon.

LORNA   Grace, the money that's paying for this.
         It, it isn't strictly mine.

         Pause.

         I wanted to be honest with you about that.
         In case you...
         Felt that I misled you.

GRACE   Okay.

LORNA   Because strictly it's Bruno's.

GRACE   Okay.

         GRACE *stands up.*

LORNA   Don't go.
         Please.

GRACE   I can't accept it, Lorna.
         You know I can't.

LORNA   But.
         He makes all this money.
         It's obscene, the amount he...
         He has nothing to spend it on, nothing of any worth.
         At least let us –

GRACE   I can't take something from a man I don't know.

LORNA   But... why not?

GRACE   You know it isn't right.

LORNA   But I so...
         I so desperately want to help and...

GRACE   It isn't fair.
         Why should I benefit?

LORNA   You deserve it.

GRACE   Why?

LORNA   You don't have to be like the women in your
         tapes.
         You don't have to just get on with it.

GRACE   Why am I any better than them?
         Better than my mum?
         Better than yours?

LORNA   No –

GRACE   They're just the idiots who sat around and let it
         happen to them?

LORNA   Don't twist my words.

GRACE   I thought it was Reza anyway.

LORNA   No.
         No he was.
         Before.
         I'm with Bruno now.

GRACE   There was another one as well, wasn't there?

LORNA   I mean, I've had boyfriends.

         Pause.

GRACE   You're still young.
         You could go and do something by yourself.
         Anything.
         Go round the world or –

LORNA   I'm happy.
         I am.
         He –
         He makes me happy.

GRACE	I've managed alright. By myself. When they're not around you can see clearer.
LORNA	I don't want to be by myself.
GRACE	Why?
LORNA	I just, I don't – I can't.
GRACE	Why?
LORNA	Please just stay and see the doctor.

GRACE bends down and kisses LORNA on the cheek.

GRACE	I know you were only trying to help.
LORNA	Please. You'll die if you don't do this.
GRACE	Call you when I'm home. Okay?

21

GRACE*'s bedroom.*

Night.

GRACE	You awake? Lorna? You awake?
LORNA	Hmm?
GRACE	I can't sleep.

Pause.

Can I show you something?

LORNA   What?

GRACE   Come here.

LORNA   What is it?

GRACE   Open it.

          Pause.

LORNA   God...

GRACE   It's nearly nine hundred pounds.

LORNA   But – ?

GRACE   I've been saving it.
          All those summers at the factory.
          Dad doesn't know...

          Pause.

          I have to get out.
          Are you listening?
          You have to listen.

LORNA   I'm listening.

GRACE   I have to, I –
          I can't stay here any more.
          Will you help me?

LORNA   Yes.

GRACE   Don't let me talk myself out of it.

LORNA   I won't.

GRACE   I'm going to get a place at university.
          Somewhere miles and miles away.

LORNA   Yes.

GRACE   We'll go together.

LORNA   Yes.

GRACE   But listen.

LORNA   I am listening.

GRACE   If I get soft-hearted.
         If I say, they can't do without me.
         Remind me of this.
         Promise?

LORNA   I promise.

GRACE   I can't always be...
         For other people, I can't.

LORNA   No.

GRACE   Even with Mike...
         I'm always...
         I give him everything.
         And he just –
         He takes it.

LORNA   Yes.

GRACE   I have to get out.
         If I don't I'm so scared I'll just...

LORNA   You won't.

GRACE   But I might.

LORNA   I won't let you.
         I promise.

GRACE   Do you feel guilty?
         I mean, do you feel guilty all the time?

LORNA   Yes.

GRACE   What about?

LORNA   Everything.
         Nothing.

GRACE   I'm so scared I'm selfish.

LORNA   You aren't.

GRACE   We have to work really hard.
         We have to be the best.

LORNA   You're much cleverer than me.

GRACE   I wish you wouldn't always say that.

LORNA   Christopher's getting me a tutor.

GRACE   Write down everything he says.
           And then show it to me.

LORNA   He costs twenty-five pounds an hour.

GRACE   I'm serious, Lorna.
           Will you?

LORNA   I'll try.

GRACE   No more parties.
           No more getting stoned by the river with Sam and
           Ted and all those wasters.
           We have to be learning.

LORNA   Alright...

GRACE   We have to.
           Do you understand?

LORNA   You don't have to give me a Chinese burn.

GRACE   Don't tell anyone.
           About the money.

LORNA   I won't.

GRACE   I'll kill you if you do.
           I'll jam a pen into your gullet.

LORNA   I know.

GRACE   Alright.
           Now go to sleep.

22

GRACE's *kitchen*.

LORNA	Comfortable?
GRACE	Ish.
LORNA	Can you see the telly alright?
GRACE	I'd rather just have the radio.
LORNA	Okay wait a minute. Better?
GRACE	You can turn the lights off as well.
LORNA	What, and sit in the dark?
GRACE	I've got candles somewhere.
LORNA	Bit morbid, isn't it?
GRACE	I've always had a taste for the dramatic.
LORNA	I feel like I'm about to do a séance.
GRACE	To be fair, there's enough people we could contact.
LORNA	Oh God. Don't.
GRACE	Is the heating on?
LORNA	The radiator's scalding.
GRACE	My temperature's all off-kilter. Sorry.

LORNA's takes GRACE's hands.

LORNA	God, your hands are cold though.
GRACE	Are they?

She rubs GRACE's fingers vigorously.

LORNA	Better?

They sit together, their hands still entwined.

Are you in lots of pain?

GRACE   I can't tell yet.
          I feel sleepy.

LORNA   Close your eyes.

GRACE   You don't have to stay.

LORNA   Yes I do.
          And anyway I'm not going to Mum's.
          We're fighting at the moment.

GRACE   Did I tell you?
          She got in touch with mine.
          The other week.

LORNA   Did she?

GRACE   They went for a coffee…
          Ow.

LORNA   Are you alright?

GRACE   Yeah in a sec…

          Pause.

          They've scraped everything out of me down there.
          Everything.

LORNA   I know.

GRACE   I'm barely a woman any more.

LORNA   That's not true.

GRACE   Remember that book I stole from your stepdad?
          'Boy/girl. Male/female.'

LORNA   You never gave it back.

GRACE   I've probably still got it somewhere.

LORNA   He moved to Manchester I think.
          I don't speak to him any more.

GRACE   He once told me I should have been born a boy.

LORNA   Did he?

GRACE   He didn't like us spending time together.
         I think he thought I was in love with you or
         something.

LORNA   He wanted everything to be fraught with sexual
         tension.

GRACE   Do you think maybe people don't understand what
         it can be like?
         That fire.
         Between two women.

LORNA   I'm not sure I understand what it was like.
         With us.

         They sit.

GRACE   Was I awful?

LORNA   No.
         Sometimes.

GRACE   You got on my nerves.
         You were always doing yourself down.
         But you were the only person I really wanted to
         hang around with.

LORNA   I was so jealous of you.

GRACE   Were you?

LORNA   Your cleverness.
         Your boldness.

GRACE   You were always much braver than me.

LORNA   You must be joking.

GRACE   I didn't have to have Martha.

LORNA   You were so young.
         How can you know what you want...

GRACE   But if I had her...
         That way I wouldn't have had to try.
         And fail.

LORNA   You'd never have failed.
         You haven't.

GRACE   I've still got that money.
         It's for her.
         When she's eighteen.

LORNA   Oh, Grace –

GRACE   Not that it's much.
         It seemed like wealth untold.
         At the time.

LORNA   I'm sorry.

GRACE   For what?

LORNA   It should have been you.
         You who got to do everything.
         I should have been the one who had to stay.

GRACE   At least one of us got to.
         And anyway we're here now.
         Back where we started.

         Pause.

         I think I'll nod off in a minute.

LORNA   I'll do the washing up.

GRACE   No.
         Don't bother.
         Martha can do it tomorrow.
         She loves doing it.
         Little weirdo.

LORNA   She's so funny.

GRACE   I'm glad she likes physics so much.
         But she does go on a bit.

LORNA   I learnt a lot earlier.

         GRACE *closes her eyes.*

GRACE   If you want to nap or anything.
         Just go and use my bed.
         I normally just curl up in this chair.
         It was Dad's.

LORNA   I'm fine here.

GRACE   Don't feel you have to sit there all night.

LORNA   Go to sleep.
         Go on.
         I'll be here.

         LORNA *looks at* GRACE.

         Watches her fall asleep.

         Did I tell you I'm single again?
         I've been single for three months.
         That's the longest ever, since I was thirteen.
         Isn't that ridiculous?
         I don't know what I was always so scared of.
         I've discovered I like being on my own.
         The cutlery drawer is so light.
         After he took all his fancy silver stuff.
         Mostly I just eat out of the saucepan now.

         She watches GRACE.

         Sometimes I worry.
         You can't not, it's sort of etched into you.
         Nearly at that moment now.
         That cliff we all fall off, apparently.
         You're so lucky, with Martha.
         I'd look after her, you know.
         If you wanted.
         I'd move back here, do whatever was right.
         Are you asleep now?
         Grace?
         Grace?

 # 23

A hill.

RUTH *and* PENNY.

They are both heavily pregnant.

RUTH	Penny?
PENNY	What?
RUTH	Slow down a bit?
PENNY	It's good for us to walk. Come on.
RUTH	She's kicking like anything.
PENNY	Exactly! Enjoying the exertion.
RUTH	Let's stop and have some tea.
PENNY	Not just yet.
RUTH	Have pity on a poor pregnant wench.
PENNY	You always make such a fuss.
RUTH	I'm stopping.
PENNY	Fine. We'll have a five-minute rest. Then we'll crack on.
RUTH	You're the size of a house.
PENNY	Speak for yourself.
RUTH	The blind leading the blind.

They sit.

There's a tiny bit left in the flask.
We could share a cup.

PENNY   No you have it.
I'm not bothered.

They sit.

Isn't it good?
To be out.
I just want to be outside all the time at the moment.

RUTH   God I don't.
          I just want my bed.

PENNY   I feel itchy everywhere.

RUTH   I had that with Ted.

PENNY   No, I don't mean like, in my skin.
          I mean like...
          I don't know.

RUTH   God, look at my ankles.
          They're disgusting.

PENNY   I can't sit still.

RUTH   You'll jiggle this tea out my hands in a second.

PENNY   I just want to keep walking.

RUTH   Aren't you knackered?

PENNY   No.

RUTH   I am.
          How long have we been going?

PENNY   Not that long.

RUTH   It would serve you right if she popped out right
          this second.

PENNY   Is she still kicking?

RUTH   Yeah, feel.

          PENNY *puts her hands on* RUTH*'s stomach.*

PENNY   Bloody hell.

RUTH   I know.

PENNY   Mine's much less acrobatic.
          I hope she won't be boring.

RUTH	I wish I'd brought Ted with me. I miss him.
PENNY	Oh, Ruth, no.
RUTH	I feel strange without him. Like I've left my purse in a shop.
PENNY	You said he was driving you mad.
RUTH	What if something's happened to him since I've been gone?
PENNY	You're being daft.
RUTH	Reg is hopeless with him.
PENNY	It will do him good to get better then.
RUTH	He'll be in a foul mood if I'm late.
PENNY	That's his problem.
RUTH	I should get back.
PENNY	Stay a bit longer.
RUTH	No. I should get back.

Pause.

PENNY	Imagine if we didn't.
RUTH	You what?
PENNY	We could just keep going. See where we ended up. We could do it, Ruth. There's nothing stopping us.
RUTH	Ha ha.
PENNY	We could find a house somewhere. Middle of nowhere. You could sneak back and kidnap Teddy. The girls and him would just run around naked. Or they'd wear each other's clothes, it wouldn't matter.

RUTH   Well, where's this house?

PENNY   Up to you.
           You pick.

RUTH   I always liked the Lakes.

PENNY   There you go.
           That's where we're headed.

RUTH   No men allowed, then?

PENNY   We'd allow them.
           But they'd have a strict time limit.
           They'd just be our playthings.

RUTH   We'd swap stories about them and laugh over their
           genitals.

PENNY   Fond laughter, though.
           We wouldn't be cruel.

RUTH   We'd swim naked in the water every morning.
           We'd have skin like rubber.

PENNY   Our toenails would be gnarled and claw-like.
           We'd barely brush our teeth.

RUTH   We'd teach our daughters to be noisy and
           confrontational.

PENNY   We'd teach them to upend everything.

RUTH   No man will ever break their hearts.

PENNY   They won't have hearts.
           They'll just have breastplates made of iron.

RUTH   They'll wear futuristic jumpsuits and shave their
           heads.

PENNY   They won't get cancer because they've had
           children, or not had children.

RUTH   They'll be kind to each other.

PENNY   They won't treat each other like competition.

RUTH   They won't ever make mistakes.
             Mistakes will be extinct!

PENNY   They'll be happy.

             Pause.

RUTH   Penny?

PENNY   What?

RUTH   What if I love Ted too much?
             What if there's not enough left for her?

PENNY   There will be.

RUTH   What if there isn't?

PENNY   Well then you'll just have to pretend.
             Help me up.

             They stand.

             Come on.

RUTH   Where are you going?

PENNY   Back.

RUTH   So that was just talk?

PENNY   No.
             Just not today.
             That's all.

             PENNY *starts to walk.*

             RUTH *stays.*

             She looks out.

             Are you coming?

             RUTH *looks out.*

RUTH   Yeah.
             Coming.

             The End.

A Nick Hern Book

Out of Love first published in Great Britain in 2017 as a paperback original by Nick Hern Books Limited, The Glasshouse, 49a Goldhawk Road, London W12 8QP, in association with Paines Plough, Theatr Clwyd and the Orange Tree Theatre, Richmond

Out of Love copyright © 2017 Elinor Cook

Elinor Cook has asserted her right to be identified as the author of this work

Cover photograph by Rebecca Need-Menear

Designed and typeset by Nick Hern Books, London
Printed and bound by CPI Group (UK) Ltd, Croydon, CR0 4YY

A CIP catalogue record for this book is available from the British Library

ISBN 978 1 84842 685 6

www.nickhernbooks.co.uk

facebook.com/nickhernbooks

twitter.com/nickhernbooks